The Perfect Lemonade Cookbook for You

Collection of Refreshing lemonade Recipes That Will Amaze Everyone

BY: Valeria Ray

License Notes

A Special Reward for Purchasing My Book!

Thank you, cherished reader, for purchasing my book and taking the time to read it. As a special reward for your decision, I would like to offer a gift of free and discounted books directly to your inbox. All you need to do is fill in the box below with your email address and name to start getting amazing offers in the comfort of your own home. You will never miss an offer because a reminder will be sent to you. Never miss a deal and get great deals without having to leave the house! Subscribe now and start saving!

SUBSCRIBE
———— TO NEWSLETTER ————

Enter your email address

https://valeria-ray.gr8.com

Contents

Refreshing lemonade Recipes

MMMMMMMMMMMMMMMMMMMMMMMMMMMMMMMMMMMM

(1) Springtime Lemonade

Here is an easy recipe that you can enjoy during the warm days of spring.

Yield: 6

Cooking Time: 10 mins.

List of Ingredients:

- 6 jasmine green tea bags
- ½-1 C. sugar
- 1 tablespoon lemon zest
- 9 C. filtered water
- 1 C. fresh lemon juice

Garnish

- mint leaves

MMMMMMMMMMMMMMMMMMMMMMMMMMMMMMMMMMM

Methods:

1. In the reserve of the coffee maker, add the water.
2. Put the unbleached filter in the coffee filter.
3. Add the sugar, tea bags and lemon zest and process until sugar is dissolved.
4. Transfer the tea into a pitcher and keep aside to cool completely.
5. Add the lemon juice and stir to combine.
6. Add enough ice cubes to fill the pitcher.
7. Transfer into ice filled glasses and enjoy with a garnishing of the mint leaves.

(2) Lemonade Tea

Who says you can only enjoy lemonade cold? Not us, here we have a tasty recipe that allows you to spin your lemonade into tea.

Yield: 8

Cooking Time: 5 mins.

List of Ingredients:

- 4 C. brewed tea
- 3 C. water
- 1 (6 oz.) cans frozen lemonade, thawed
- ¼ C. sugar
- 1 teaspoon almond extract

MMMMMMMMMMMMMMMMMMMMMMMMMMMMMMMMMM

Methods:

1. In a pitcher, add all the ingredients and stir until well combined.
2. Transfer into ice filled glasses and enjoy.

(3) Creamy Lemonade

The mixture of condensed milk and lemonade mix makes a creamy masterpiece.

Yield: 4

Cooking Time: 10 mins.

List of Ingredients:

- 2 limes, wedges
- ½ C. sugar
- 3 tablespoons milk, sweetened condensed
- 3 C. water
- ice

MMMMMMMMMMMMMMMMMMMMMMMMMMMMMMMM

Methods:

1. In a food processor, add the sugar, limes, water, condensed milk and ice and pulse until smooth.
2. Through a sieve, strain the mixture, pressing with the back of a spoon.
3. Transfer into ice filled glasses and enjoy.

(4) Hawaiian Lemonade Pie

This delicious pie is so refreshing that it is perfect for a hot day.

Yield: 6

Cooking Time: 20 mins.

List of Ingredients:

- 1 (16 oz.) cans frozen pink lemonade concentrate, thawed
- 1 C. sweetened condensed milk
- 1 (8 oz.) cartons Cool Whip
- 1 (9 inch) graham cracker crust

MMMMMMMMMMMMMMMMMMMMMMMMMMMMMMMMMM

Methods:

1. In a bowl, add all the ingredients except the pie crust and mix until smooth.
2. Place the mixture into the prepared pie shell and freeze overnight.

(5) Ontario Lemonade

Take a trip to Canada with this amazing glass of Ontario Lemonade.

Yield: 1

Cooking Time: 5 mins.

List of Ingredients:

- 3 (4 g) packets of crystal light lemonade
- 3 (12 oz.) cans of fizzy water
- basil leaves, torn
- fresh ginger, grated

MMMMMMMMMMMMMMMMMMMMMMMMMMMMMMMM

Methods:

1. In a pitcher, add all the ingredients and mix well.
2. Transfer into ice filled glasses and enjoy.

(6) Georgia Lemonade

Transport yourself to Atlanta with every sip of this delicious drink.

Yield: 4

Cooking Time: 20 mins.

List of Ingredients:

- 2 peaches, peeled and chopped
- 1 C. granulated sugar
- 4 C. water
- ¾ C. squeezed lemon juice
- mint sprig
- peach slices

MMMMMMMMMMMMMMMMMMMMMMMMMMMMMMMMMMM

Methods:

1. In a pan, add the sugar, peaches and water and cook until boiling.
2. Now, set the heat to low and cook for about 10 minutes, stirring frequently.
3. Remove from the heat and keep aside to cool completely.
4. Through a fine mesh strainer, strain the mixture into a pitcher, pressing with the back of a spoon to extract all the juice.
5. Add the lemon juice and stir to combine well.
6. Transfer into serving ice filled glasses evenly.
7. Enjoy with a garnishing of the mint and peach slices.

(7) Heirloom Kitchen Lemonade

Give yourself a treat with this delicious glass of lemonade.

Yield: 6

Cooking Time: 11 mins.

List of Ingredients:

- 1 C. unbleached white sugar
- ½ C. filtered water
- 1 tablespoon grated ginger
- 1 tablespoon chopped fresh grown lemon verbena plant leaves
- 1 C. blueberries
- ½ C. fresh lemon juice
- 4 C. filtered water

MMMMMMMMMMMMMMMMMMMMMMMMMMMMMMM

Methods:

1. In a pan, add the lemon verbena, ginger, ½ C. of the sugar and ½ C. of the water and cook for about 2 minutes, stirring continuously.
2. Remove from the heat and place the sugar syrup into a container.
3. Refrigerate, covered to chill before using.
4. In a food processor, add the remaining ½ C. of the sugar and blueberries and pulse until smooth.
5. Add the remaining water and lemon juice and pulse until well combined.
6. In a bowl, add the chilled syrup and blueberry mixture and mix well.
7. Through a strainer, strain the mixture into a pitcher.
8. Transfer into ice filled glasses and enjoy with the whole fresh lemon verbena leaves.

(8) Lime and Mango Lemonade

This delicious lemonade will take you to the tropics with its refreshing flavors of mango and lime.

Yield: 1

Cooking Time: 15 mins.

List of Ingredients:

- 2 C. chopped mangoes, pureed
- 5 C. cold water
- ½ C. fresh lime juice
- 1 ½ C. sugar

MMMMMMMMMMMMMMMMMMMMMMMMMMMMMMMMMMM

Methods:

1. In a pitcher, add the dissolved sugar, mango puree and water and mix well.
2. Add the lime juice and stir to combine.
3. Transfer into ice filled glasses and enjoy.

(9) Harvest Moon Lemonade

This mixture is minty, fruity and sweet.

Yield: 4

Cooking Time: 15 mins.

List of Ingredients:

- 1 C. water
- ½ C. granulated sugar
- ½ C. fresh mint leaves, packed
- 3 kiwi fruits, peeled and cut into chunks
- 2 -3 lemons, juiced
- sparkling water

MMMMMMMMMMMMMMMMMMMMMMMMMMMMMMMMMM

Methods:

1. Place the sugar and water in a pot over medium-high heat and cook until sugar dissolves completely, stirring often.
2. Now, set the heat to low and cook for about 4 minutes, mixing time to time.
3. Remove from the heat and immediately, mix the mint leaves.
4. Keep aside for about 20 minutes.
5. In a blender, add the kiwifruit and pulse until pureed.
6. In a pitcher, place the pureed kiwi.
7. Through a strainer, strain the cooled syrup into the pitcher, pressing with the back of a spoon.
8. Place the pitcher in fridge to chill.
9. Add the lemon juice and stir to combine.
10. Transfer into serving glasses and enjoy with a garnishing of the kiwi slices.

(10) Persian Lemonade

The addition of rose water to this refreshing drink makes all the difference on a hot day.

Yield: 6

Cooking Time: 1 hour 5 mins.

List of Ingredients:

- 5 1/3 C. water
- 1 C. granulated sugar
- 1 1/3 C. fresh lemon juice
- 2 ½-3 ½ teaspoons rose water

MMMMMMMMMMMMMMMMMMMMMMMMMMMMMMMMMM

Methods:

1. In a pan, add the sugar and water over medium-low heat and cook until sugar dissolves, stirring continuously.
2. Remove from the heat and keep aside to cool completely.
3. Transfer the cooled sugar syrup into a pitcher with the lemon juice and rose water and mix well.
4. Place in the fridge to chill completely.
5. Enjoy chilled.

(11) Lemon Lemonade Cupcakes

These delicious cupcakes are light, airy and fluffy with the taste of pink lemonade.

Yield: 10

Cooking Time: 35 mins.

List of Ingredients:

Cakes

- 1 C. all-purpose flour
- ½ teaspoons baking powder
- ¼ teaspoons baking soda
- 1 pinch salt
- ½ C. granulated sugar
- ¼ C. canola oil
- 2 egg whites
- 1/3 C. frozen pink lemonade concentrate, thawed
- ¼ C. buttermilk
- 3 drops red food coloring

Frosting

- 1 ½ C. icing sugar, sifted to remove lumps
- ½ C. unsalted butter
- 1 pinch salt
- ¼ C. whipping cream
- 2 teaspoons frozen pink lemonade concentrate, thawed
- 1 teaspoon lemon extract
- 3 drops red food coloring

Methods:

1. Set your oven to 375 degrees F before doing anything else and line 10 cups of a muffin pan with the paper liners.

2. In a bowl, add the flour, baking soda, baking powder and salt and mix well.

3. In another bowl, add the lemonade concentrate, oil, sugar and egg whites and beat until smooth.

4. Add the flour mixture in three additions alternately with the buttermilk and beat until just combined.

5. Add the food coloring and stir to combine.

6. Transfer the mixture into the prepared muffin cups evenly.

7. Cook in the oven for about 20-25 minutes or until a toothpick inserted in the center comes out clean.

8. Remove from the oven and keep onto the wire rack to cool in the pan for about 5-10 minutes.

9. Carefully, invert the cupcakes onto the wire rack to cool completely.

10. Meanwhile, for the frosting: in a bowl, add the butter, sugar and salt and with an electric mixer, beat on low speed until creamy.

11. Now, beat on high speed until fluffy.

12. Add the lemon extract and lemonade concentrate and beat until well combined.

13. Add the cream and beat until fluffy.

14. Spread the frosting over the cooled cupcakes and enjoy.

(12) 2-Berry Lemonade

This berry lemonade has the right amount of sweetness with the perfect level of zest.

Yield: 1

Cooking Time: 5 mins.

List of Ingredients:

- ½ kiwi
- 3 medium strawberries
- 1 lemon
- ½ C. water
- 1 -1 ½ tablespoons sugar
- 2 ice cubes

MMMMMMMMMMMMMMMMMMMMMMMMMMMMMMMMM

Methods:

1. With your hands, squeeze the strawberries and kiwi into bowl.
2. Squeeze the lemons in the bowl with a lemon squeezer.
3. Add the sugar and water and stir until sugar is dissolved.
4. Enjoy.

(13) Apple Lemonade

This lemonade has a nice hint of apple that makes it even more delicious.

Yield: 8

Cooking Time: 10

List of Ingredients:

- 1 ¼ C. lemon juice
- ¾ C. sugar
- 6 C. apple juice, unsweetened
- 1 C. water

MMMMMMMMMMMMMMMMMMMMMMMMMMMMMMMMM

Methods:

1. In a food processor, add the sugar, ½ C. of the apple juice and lemon juice and pulse until well combined.
2. Keep aside or about 8-10 minutes.
3. Now, pulse for about 30-40 seconds.
4. Add 2 C. apple juice and the ice and pulse on low until well combined.
5. In a pitcher, place the mixture with the remaining apple juice and mix well.
6. Enjoy.

(14) North Carolina Style Lemonade

Continuing on our tour around the world of lemonade we have an amazingly refreshing drink that will transport you to North Carolina.

Yield: 1

Cooking Time: 20 mins.

List of Ingredients:

- 1/3 C. fresh lemon juice
- 2 C. water
- 2 C. fresh blueberries
- ½ C. sugar

MMMMMMMMMMMMMMMMMMMMMMMMMMMMMMMMM

Methods:

1. In a food processor, add all the ingredients and pulse until smooth.
2. With a fine mesh strainer, strain the mixture into a pitcher.
3. Transfer into ice filled glasses and enjoy.

(15) French Lemonade

Enjoy a nice exotic glass of lemonade using this easy recipe.

Yield: 4

Cooking Time: 30 mins.

List of Ingredients:

- 1 C. sugar
- 5 C. water, divided
- 1 tablespoon dried lavender
- 1 C. fresh-squeezed lemon juice

MMMMMMMMMMMMMMMMMMMMMMMMMMMMMMMMM

Methods:

1. In a pot, add the 2 C. of the water and sugar and cook until boiling, stirring continuously.
2. Add the lavender and stir to combine.
3. Remove from the heat and keep aside, covered for about 1-2 hours.
4. Through a strain, strain the mixture into a pitcher.
5. Add remaining 2 C. of the water and lemon juice and mix well.
6. Transfer into ice filled glasses and enjoy with the garnishing of the fresh lavender flowers.

(16) Country Fruit Lemonade

This drink is fruity, rich and delicious.

Yield: 1

Cooking Time: 10 mins.

List of Ingredients:

- 24 oz. frozen lemonade concentrate, thawed
- 2 liters club soda, chilled
- 20 oz. frozen sweetened raspberries, thawed
- 2 -4 tablespoons sugar
- ice cube

MMMMMMMMMMMMMMMMMMMMMMMMMMMMMMMMM

Methods:

1. In a food processor, add the sugar, raspberries and lemonade concentrate and pulse until well combined.
2. Through a strainer, strain the mixture, pressing with the back of a spoon.
3. In a large pitcher, add the club soda, raspberry mixture and ice cubes and stir to combine well.
4. Enjoy.

(17) Lemonade Tunisian

This recipe is easy and tasty.

Yield: 6

Cooking Time: 5 mins.

List of Ingredients:

- 8 lemons, juiced
- ¾ C. sugar
- 1 teaspoon orange blossom water
- ¼ C. chopped mint
- water
- ice cube

MMMMMMMMMMMMMMMMMMMMMMMMMMMMMMMMMMMM

Methods:

1. In a pitcher, add the lemon juice and sugar and stir until dissolved.
2. Add the mint and orange blossom water and stir to combine well.
3. Divide the lemonade into serving glasses and fill with the ice and water.
4. Enjoy.

(18) Caribbean Style Lemonade

Get transported to the islands with this tropical delight.

Yield: 8

Cooking Time: 15 mins.

List of Ingredients:

- 1 C. sugar
- 1 C. boiling water
- 3 ½ C. cold water, divided
- 3 C. peeled chopped papayas
- 1 C. fresh lemon juice

MMMMMMMMMMMMMMMMMMMMMMMMMMMMMMMM

Methods:

1. In a bowl, add the boiling water and sugar and mix until sugar is dissolved completely.
2. Keep aside to cool for about 4-5 minutes.
3. In a food processor, add the papaya, sugar syrup, lemon juice and 2 C. of the cold water and pulse until smooth.
4. Transfer the mixture into a pitcher with the remaining cold water and stir to combine.
5. Transfer into ice filled glasses and enjoy.

(19) Mango Lemonade

The mixture of mango and lime in this recipe is phenomenal.

Yield: 4

Cooking Time: 2 mins.

List of Ingredients:

- 3 large ripe mangoes, peeled and seeded
- ½ C. sugar
- 2 tablespoons lime juice
- 2 ½ C. water
- 1 C. lemon juice

MMMMMMMMMMMMMMMMMMMMMMMMMMMMMMMM

Methods:

1. In a food processor, add the sugar and mangoes and pulse until smooth.
2. Transfer the pureed mango mixture into a pitcher.
3. Add the lemon juice and water and stir to combined.
4. Enjoy chilled.

(20) Lemonade Cake

Now you can spin your lemonade into a delicate cake with this easy recipe.

Yield: 10

Cooking Time: 1 hr. 3 mins.

List of Ingredients:

- 1 (15 oz.) packages yellow cake mix
- 1 (3 oz.) packages Jell-O vanilla
- 4 oz. country time lemonade mix, divided
- 1 C. cold water
- 4 eggs
- ¼ C. oil
- 3 tablespoons warm water
- 1 C. powdered sugar

MMMMMMMMMMMMMMMMMMMMMMMMMMMMMM

Methods:

1. Set your oven to 350 degrees F before doing anything else and grease and flour a fluted tube pan.

2. In a bowl, add the ¼ C. of the drink mix, pudding mix, cake mix, oil, eggs and 1 C. of the water and with an electric mixer, beat on low speed for about 1 minute.

3. Now, set the mixer on medium speed and beat for about 4 minutes.

4. Transfer the mixture into the prepared tube pan evenly.

5. Cook in the oven for about 50-55 minutes or until a toothpick inserted in the center comes out clean.

6. Remove from the oven and keep onto the wire rack to cool in the pan for about 10 minutes.

7. Carefully, invert the cake onto a platter.

8. Meanwhile, for the glaze: in a bowl, add the remaining ¼ C. of the drink and 3 tablespoons of the warm water and mix until well combined.

9. Add the powdered sugar and beat until well combined.

10. With a fork, poke the warm cake at many places about 1-inch apart.

11. Place the glaze over the warm cake and keep aside until glaze absorbs completely.

(21) 3-Ingredient Lemonade-Tea

This lemonade is so easy to whip up that it just has 3 ingredients.

Yield: 8

Cooking Time: 35 mins.

List of Ingredients:

- 5 bags tea
- 1 quart water
- 1 C. sweetened strawberry-lemonade drink mix

MMMMMMMMMMMMMMMMMMMMMMMMMMMMMMMMMMM

Methods:

1. In a pan, add the water and tea bags and cook until boiling.
2. Keep aside for about 35-40 minutes.
3. In a pitcher, add the tea and drink mix and mix until well combined.
4. Add enough cold water to fill the pitcher.
5. Enjoy.

(22) Black Tea Lemonade

Combine your tea and lemons to create this brilliant glass of deliciousness.

Yield: 4

Cooking Time: 20 mins.

List of Ingredients:

- ¾ C. Splenda granular
- 1 tablespoon grated fresh ginger root
- 12 allspice berries
- 8 whole cloves
- 4 black tea bags
- 2/3 C. lemon juice
- 2 unpeeled oranges, sliced

MMMMMMMMMMMMMMMMMMMMMMMMMMMMMMMMMMMM

Methods:

1. In a pot, add the 1 C. of water, ginger root, sugar, allspice and cloves over medium heat and cook until boiling, stirring continuously.
2. Set the heat to low and cook for about 4-5 minutes.
3. Remove from the heat and stir in the teabags.
4. Keep aside, covered for about 6 minutes.
5. Through a fine mesh strainer, strain into a pitcher.
6. Add the orange juice, lemon juice and 3 C. of the cold water and with the back of a spoon, crush the oranges slightly.
7. Transfer into ice filled glasses and enjoy.

(23) Blood Orange Lemonade

This lemonade is rich, tangy and delicious.

Yield: 10

Cooking Time: 10 mins.

List of Ingredients:

- 8 C. water
- 1 C. sugar
- 2 blood oranges, juice
- 2 lemons, juice
- 1 teaspoon orange blossom water

MMMMMMMMMMMMMMMMMMMMMMMMMMMMMMM

Methods:

1. In a pitcher, add the sugar and water and mix until sugar is dissolved.
2. Add orange juice, lemon juice and blossom water and mix well.
3. Refrigerate to chill completely.
4. Transfer into ice filled glasses and enjoy.

(24) Early Autumn Lemonade

Finally, a lemonade for Fall that will rehydrate your soul.

Yield: 6

Cooking Time: 15 mins.

List of Ingredients:

- 10 -12 medium lemons, scrubbed well, halved
- 3 tablespoons grated fresh ginger
- 1 ¼ C. granulated sugar
- 1 pinch salt
- 5 C. cold water

MMMMMMMMMMMMMMMMMMMMMMMMMMMMMMMMMMMM

Methods:

1. In a bowl, add the sugar, salt, ginger and lemons and with a wooden spoon, crush for about 5 minutes.
2. Through a strainer, strain the syrup and lemon slices in 2 batches, pressing with the back of a spoon.
3. In a pitcher, add the lemon mixture and water and mix well.
4. Refrigerate until chilled completely.
5. Transfer into ice filled glasses and enjoy.

(25) 4th Grade Lemonade

This lemonade is so easy that it could be whipped up by a 4th grader.

Yield: 1

Cooking Time: 5 mins.

List of Ingredients:

- 1 (12 oz.) cans lemonade concentrate
- water
- ¼ C. chocolate syrup

MMMMMMMMMMMMMMMMMMMMMMMMMMMMMMMMMMM

Methods:

1. In a pitcher, add the water and lemonade concentrate and mix well.
2. Add the chocolate syrup and stir to combine well.
3. Transfer into ice filled glasses and enjoy.

(26) Orange Blossom Lemonade

Integrate our orange blossoms into this amazingly easy lemonade recipe.

Yield: 1

Cooking Time: 15 mins.

List of Ingredients:

- 1 C. water
- 1 large lemon, juiced
- 1 tablespoon honey
- 1 small dashes orange blossom water

MMMMMMMMMMMMMMMMMMMMMMMMMMMMMMMMMM

Methods:

1. In a pitcher, add all the ingredients and mix until well combined.
2. Refrigerate until chilled completely.
3. Transfer into ice filled glasses and enjoy.

(27) Lemonade Muffins

These muffins are so lemony and delicious that your kids will fall in love with them.

Yield: 8

Cooking Time: 40 mins.

List of Ingredients:

- 1 ½ C. flour
- ¼ C. sugar
- 2 ½ teaspoons baking powder
- ½ teaspoons salt
- 1 beaten egg
- 1 (6 oz.) cans frozen lemonade, thawed
- ¼ C. milk
- 1/3 C. cooking oil
- ½ C. chopped walnuts

MMMMMMMMMMMMMMMMMMMMMMMMMMMMMM

Methods:

1. Set your oven to 375 degrees F before doing anything else and grease 8-9 cups of a large muffin pan.
2. In a bowl, add the flour, sugar, baking powder and salt and mix well.
3. In a separate bowl, add the milk, oil, egg and ½ C. of the lemonade and beat until well combined.
4. Add the egg mixture into the flour mixture and mix until just combined.
5. Fold in the walnuts.
6. Transfer the mixture into the prepared muffin cups evenly.
7. Cook in the oven for about 15-20 minutes or until a toothpick inserted in the center comes out clean.
8. Remove from the oven and keep onto the wire rack to cool in the pan for about 5 minutes.
9. Carefully, invert the muffins onto the wire rack.
10. Coat the muffins with the remaining lemonade evenly.
11. Enjoy with the dusting of white sugar.

(28) Virginia State Lemonade

This lemonade recipe is popular among college students as it is very easy to whip up yet delicious.

Yield: 1

Cooking Time: 17 mins.

List of Ingredients:

- 4 C. water
- 1 C. sugar
- 1 C. lemon juice
- 1 tablespoon grated lemon peel
- 1 C. blackberry
- 1 -2 drop blue food coloring

MMMMMMMMMMMMMMMMMMMMMMMMMMMMMMMMM

Methods:

1. In a pan, add the sugar and 2 C. of the water and cook until boiling, mixing frequently.
2. Cook for about 3 minutes.
3. Remove from the heat and stir in the lemon peel, lemon juice and remaining 2 C. of the water.
4. Keep aside to cool for some time.
5. In a food processor, add the blackberries and 1 C. of the lemon mixture and pulse until well combined.
6. Through a strainer, strain the mixture into a pitcher.
7. In a pitcher, add the blackberries and remaining lemon mixture and food coloring and stir to combine well.
8. Refrigerate until chilled completely.
9. Transfer into ice filled glasses and enjoy.

(29) Orange Lemonade

This citrusy mix is perfect for starting the day.

Yield: 5

Cooking Time: 3 hrs. 5 mins.

List of Ingredients:

- 3 tea bags tag and string removed
- 3 C. boiling water
- 1 (12 oz.) cans frozen lemonade concentrate
- 1 teaspoon orange extract

MMMMMMMMMMMMMMMMMMMMMMMMMMMMMMMMMM

Methods:

1. In a pitcher, add the water and tea bags and keep aside, covered for about 12-15 minutes.
2. Add the orange extract and lemonade concentrate and mix well.
3. Add enough cold water to fill the pitcher.
4. Refrigerate for about 4-5 hours.
5. Transfer into ice filled glasses and enjoy.

(30) Vanilla Lemonade Ice Cream Pie

Here is a delicious ice cream pie that can be made for your average lemonade mix.

Yield: 10

Times: 10 mins.

List of Ingredients:

- 1/3 C. country time lemonade mix
- ½ C. water
- 1 pint vanilla ice cream
- 1 (8 oz.) containers Cool Whip
- 1 (9 oz.) graham cracker pie crust

MMMMMMMMMMMMMMMMMMMMMMMMMMMMMMMM

Methods:

1. In a pitcher, add the lemonade and water and with a long wooden spoon, stir to combine well.
2. Add the ice cream and with the soon, mix until smooth.
3. Now, place the Cool Whip and mix until well blended.
4. In a prepared pie crust, place the lemonade mixture and place in the freeze for about 5 hours.

About the Author

A native of Indianapolis, Indiana, Valeria Ray found her passion for cooking while she was studying English Literature at Oakland City University. She decided to try a cooking course with her friends and the experience changed her forever. She enrolled at the Art Institute of Indiana which offered extensive courses in the culinary Arts. Once Ray dipped her toe in the cooking world, she never looked back.

When Valeria graduated, she worked in French restaurants in the Indianapolis area until she became the head chef at one of the 5-star establishments in the area. Valeria's attention to taste and visual detail caught the eye of a local business person who expressed an interest in publishing her recipes. Valeria began her secondary career authoring cookbooks and e-books which she tackled with as much talent and gusto as her first career. Her passion for food leaps off the page of her books which have colourful anecdotes and stunning pictures of dishes she has prepared herself.

Valeria Ray lives in Indianapolis with her husband of 15 years, Tom, her daughter, Isobel and their loveable Golden Retriever, Goldy. Valeria enjoys cooking special dishes in her large, comfortable kitchen where the family gets involved in preparing meals. This successful, dynamic chef is an inspiration to culinary students and novice cooks everywhere.

•••••••••• ● ● ● ● ● ● ● •••••••

Author's Afterthoughts

Thank you for Purchasing my book and taking the time to read it from front to back. I am always grateful when a reader chooses my work and I hope you enjoyed it!

With the vast selection available online, I am touched that you chose to be purchasing my work and take valuable time out of your life to read it. My hope is that you feel you made the right decision.

I very much would like to know what you thought of the book. Please take the time to write an honest and informative review on Amazon.com. Your experience and opinions will be of great benefit to me and those readers looking to make an informed choice.

With much thanks,

Valeria Ray

Made in the USA
Middletown, DE
01 March 2021